BRANDTICITY

ALTIMESE NICHOLE

Copyright © 2018 by Altimese Nichole Enterprise, LLC

www.altimesenichole.com

Cover design by Ariel J Designs

Editing Services by Write The Vision Creative Works, LLC

Book Formatting Services by Margery Walshaw

ISBN: 978-1-7324115-0-0

Library of Congress Control Number: 2018908079

This book is dedicated to my beautiful daughter Ayana (My Bella). Your presence has shown me so much beauty, faith and hope. Your life is the physical form of spiritual restoration and I am grateful for the opportunity to love you for the rest of my life.

My generation will shift the direction of our family and your generation will carry the torch of a new foundation.

Your father and I love you with all our hearts.

ACKNOWLEDGMENTS

There are so many people who poured love and support into my life while I pushed to complete this project. First and foremost, I must acknowledge Christ. I often hear people ask me how I finished a book while caring for a newborn. It truly was by the grace of God. If I try to make sense of it on my own, it simply doesn't make sense. He is my "secret sauce."

The journey of life hasn't always been easy but I have the best person by my side. Chris, you are my husband, best friend, lover, and partner. Thank you for putting up with me through this process! Your love and unconditional support means the world to me and I love you beyond words.

I would also like to thank Shelia Hampton, my second mom. Not only did you speak life into my soul, you also pushed me out of my comfort zone and reminded me that I was designed for this very moment. Thank you for your love, prayers, advice, and wisdom. You're a living example of the Proverbs 31 woman and I am so grateful one of my closest friends on this earth didn't mind sharing you with me!

Shelita, Vikkie, Ariel, Jackie, Nicole and Ashley, you all have been my biggest cheerleaders. Thank you for your encouragement and love! I'm so blessed to call you all sister-friends!

Additionally, a very special thank you to all of my friends and family who pour support into my life daily! All of you are the real MVP's!

Thank you for believing in me.

———

INTRODUCTION

I've learned to always start with *why*. Consequently, my motive remained top of mind as I wrote this book. Life happens so, deadlines were pushed, and some weren't met, but my reason for writing propelled me forward.

I started my career when brands first began to pay attention to social media, though many brand leaders were unsure of social media's overall stability at the time. Because of this, social media was often an afterthought and not yet deemed a necessity. I was blessed to be one of many millennials coming into the workforce with a skill set that I gained simply due to my generations' frequent usage of Myspace, BlackPlanet, AIM, and of course—Facebook as mediums of communication.

My solid knowledge and comfort with social media became my greatest career asset among my team members. As others began to take notice of my skills, I began to become more proactive toward investing in my craft. I returned to school for a master's degree and took numerous classes to learn more about Google Analytics, digital marketing trends, and more! I am very much *like you*. I became hungry for learning more about the business of social media and made myself available for all possible opportunities that came so I would strengthen my expertise, and as a result, I now get the pleasure of serving as a conduit to release this expertise to you! My *brandticity* is hinged upon my faith in God and relationship with Christ as my foundation and internal compass. Everything I do is connected to this relationship, as are the words written in this book. Meditation on Christ's teachings has revealed to me the importance of nurturing close relationships, while developing new ones. I am disclosing for the purpose of sharing my internal compass as an example-your internal compass may be different-- and that's okay (as long as you have identified the foundation for your internal *navigation system*). As you peruse the pages of this book, I hope that you will understand how to better navigate your own relationships while you continue to develop your personal brand with authenticity. Whether family, other loved ones, friends and social networks - relationships matter, and knowing how to manage those relationships (and platforms) matter also. I encourage you to determine what your *brandticity* will be hinged upon as you initiate this journey!

This book's intent is not to sway you in any way, aside from keeping authenticity at the forefront of your personal and professional branding. I hope this book helps you discover many wonderful things about your brand. I truly applaud you for picking up this book and I appreciate your support! Stay hungry for knowledge and never stop learning.

Altimese Nichole

THE FOUNDATION OF BRANDING

Within the last 20 years, technology has completely changed the routine of our lives. Prior to the world wide web, it was expected that children play outside (coming in before the streetlights came on), families ate dinner together at the table uninterrupted, and the landline phone was the primary form of communicating with a friend that lived miles away. It was either the landline phone or mailing a handwritten letter through the postal service.

Now, things have completely changed with the help of the Internet and the advancement of technology. We can now connect with friends from childhood simply by scrolling through our time-lines on Facebook and never actually hear their voice. Children are provided tablets as young as two years old to keep them occupied, and schools are beginning the standard of providing every child a laptop instead of school books. A portion of our lives can literally play out before others through our status updates and latest pictures. Our communication styles have become deeply intertwined with social media and unfortunately, there is no going back to how *it used to be.* This is a hard reality for some and an embraced truth for others. No matter which side of the coin you're on, we're all faced with the same foundation of certainty: social conversations are here to stay forever.

As we adapt to *the new normal* (which may come easier to younger generations due to exposure), it has become harder and harder to recognize truth from the superficial. Facebook connections have tarnished the perception of friendships because we now have *Facebook Friends* that are digitally connected yet have no *real* connection outside of the computer screen. Instagram likes have become more important than nurturing the relationships with our families. Snapchat's one-time videos have given us a false sense of security to do or say things that we wouldn't dare do in our real lives-especially if others knew about it.

We have shifted from wanting to build more authentic relation-ships to wanting to build a greater following on social media. We want those followers so badly we will pay for them and when we choose to build the communities through organic reach, we're faced with the challenge of algorithms and aggregated automation. Not only has it jaded the personal connection, but it has also diluted our willingness to be open, transparent, and beautifully flawed human beings.

Amid this technological evolution, intended to build bridges between physical miles and oceans, we have collectively become skilled at signaling skeptic viewpoints towards others, while simulta-neously guarding our own authenticity from these same individuals. We've created this cycle of superficial personas that lead to great inse-curity, envy, comparison, and watered-down facades. The very thing we crave from the world has become the very thing we fear to give from within ourselves:

Authenticity-being who we are truly designed to be.

PERSONAL
BRANDING:
OWNING THE
PERSONAL
BRANDING OF
YOU.

PERSONAL BRANDING

PERSONAL BRANDING GOES BEYOND THE CREATION OF FACEBOOK posts, Instagram likes, Twitter retweets and Snapchat views. Although social media is an effective tool to build a brand and presence for yourself, it's certainly not the only, or most important outlet, or avenue for creating a personal brand.

We're all aware of traditional brands. We know the brands we see and hear on television or the radio but are you aware that you're a brand as well? Every day, when you wake up, get dressed, go to work, interact with colleagues, friends and family, spend quality time defining your dreams-- all these reflect *you*. People begin to have a perception of you based upon these things.

Are you faithful to the things and people you've committed to? Are you trustworthy? Do you dress fashionably? Do you arrive to personal and professional appointments promptly?

We represent someone or something every day. With every piece of clothing, word spoken, and online comment; we're an ambassador and representative for brands, our friends, our current employers, our families, our parents, and especially ourselves!

Your personal brand is simply how you present yourself to others and exudes from the characteristics that others mentally associate with you at first thought. As you think of your branding on social media, first think of your personal brand in real life. The two should align perfectly with very little discrepancies. People in real life should not be confused by your online presence and vice versa.

Have you noticed I wrote "real life" as if social media isn't real? There is a reason for this; *it's not*. Social media is a controllable platform to connect human lives. It's not a living, breathing mechanism. It needs us to make it a part of reality. Never confuse what you see on social media as a full picture of anyone's life. While social media certainly plays a part into perception (which portrays reality) it is not, nor does it represent, the essence of the full gift of life. I will discuss this further along in the book.

YOUR CURRENT BRANDING

How we present ourselves to the world matters. According to *Business Insider*, people tend to make a swift judgement and assessment of how they "perceive" you to be within the first seven seconds of meeting you. Online, the time is omitted, and the assessment occurs immediately. Additionally, when considering social media, most people are not intentional about posts, updates, and the content shared. Most people create social media pages and use them to share opinions, feelings -- *basically the things they will not say and do in real life.*

Hiding behind the computer screen has become the newest form of passive aggression and bullying, regardless of age. This is an unfortunate reality of the world we live in today. People now use the

Internet as their personal thought journals, yet shy away from openly standing behind what they say online once it is illuminated for question, criticism, or concern. While there is nothing wrong with, and there is value in, sharing your true feelings on social media, we must all be prepared for the reactions that follow and continue to own our truths. This is where authenticity comes into action! Without a core determination to stay true to who you are, it will be easy to sway back and forth on opinions, debates, positioning, and statements.

Be unapologetic about who you present to the world, it is essential to success online, and in life overall! This simply means owning all your *stuff*. It requires becoming self-aware of your shortcomings or flaws, embracing them as you work on them, and being proud of the person you are--- *all of you*-- regardless of what others think.

As you continue reading this book, think of your current social media profiles, the messages you share, and the perceptions they could potentially create.

Here are some things to consider:

- Does my social media presence represent the core of who I am?
- Do the things I share appear to be helpful, inspiring, or thoughtful?
- Do I post when I am emotionally charged (i.e., extremely overjoyed, angry, or frustrated)?
- If someone met me after viewing my social media presence, would they feel a disconnect between who I am online and who I am in person?
- If my employer had access to my profile, would it impact how people perceive me at work-- or potentially affect my employment?
- If financial institutions made business decisions based upon social media , would my online presence positively or negatively impact the institution's decision-making process?

Little Known Fact: Some financial institutions already assess social media prior to offering specific loans to potential clients.

THESE QUESTIONS WILL HELP YOU ASSESS YOUR CURRENT *personal* brand positioning, as related to your social media profiles. Just as companies have brand reputations to uphold, every individual has the same opportunity and responsibility-all thanks to social media, of course!

THE LOST CHARACTERISTIC OF INTEGRITY

IT'S CRITICAL TO REMEMBER WE ATTRACT WHAT WE ARE. IF you're constantly surrounded by individuals that rarely keep their commitments or never live up to their own expectations in life, you may want to consider evaluating your internal characteristics and the energy you give out to others. It's impossible to give others what we don't have within, and it's unrealistic to expect others to adhere to a standard we don't govern our own selves by.

Answer the following questions:

- What does integrity mean to you?
- Does it involve your reputation or what others think of you?
- Is it something that you value in others?
- Do you value integrity within yourself?

Perhaps you're thinking, "What does this have to do with social media?"

My response, "Everything."

Webster's dictionary defines integrity as *a firm adherence (or faithful attachment) to a code of especially moral or artistic values.* With social media, apps, and the Internet at our fingertips, we have access to any and everything we can think of (with the help of Google on our phone screens). After the mere inspiration of a thought, we are able to research any topic, thing, or person, with the click of a button-- and it's just that easy!

This can be an amazingly wonderful thing; it can also be a very dangerous thing if we're not mindful of our pitfalls or weaknesses. You may think no one sees you, and it may be true now, but what's done in the dark always comes to the light.

For example, your likes on Instagram are not private. All your followers can review your recent activity by simply *following their hearts.* What does this mean? Simply, click the heart that describes recent activity on your profile. There are two tabs located in this section of the app. One labeled "YOU" and another labeled "FOL-LOWING." By clicking the *Following* tab, you can see the latest interaction of others that you follow. This is actually used for marketing techniques and to increase real-time engagement. On the contrary, it can also expose the things many think or consider to be private interactions on the Instagram app.

We can all get caught up in things that we can't dig ourselves out of if we're not careful. These types of situations normally present themselves behind closed doors when we presume no one will ever know. We begin to believe a facade that if we cover our tracks well enough, it will never be shared with others. Even worse - we never consider the hard work we've put in to get to where we are or the potential of who we might become. Don't fall into this trap. Don't live a public life to be praised and a private life that can bring shame with a simple screenshot. If your marriage, children, goals, or beliefs aren't enough to uphold a standard of integrity, do it to prove to yourself that you can and will.

"What does this have to do with branding and social media?" you ask. Apps are never fully secure; Snapchat videos are not immune to screenshots, and not everyone will keep your business private. Social media is the engine for creating a brand extension of you. Who you say you are in real life should always align with who you portray yourself to be online (in both professional and personal discussions).

DON'T LET
SOCIAL MEDIA
KILL YOUR
INTEGRITY.

Now, ONE WOULD THINK UNFILTERED AUTHENTICITY MEANS TO share anything, everything, anytime, anyplace, on any platform. This is the furthest thing from the truth. Because of this reason, it will not be of focus in this book. Unfiltered authenticity does involve integrity. Integrity matters and the appearance of your actions matter. Again, social media only portrays a snapshot of your life; however, whether you like it or not, you will be judged according to what you post online. Yes, there is a time and a place for venting on the Internet. And, yes, social media is a platform where many come together amongst common interests. But, always remember the world wide web is just that! Assume, regardless of privacy settings, whatever you access via the Internet is fair game for anyone to see. So, post wisely.

For example, I know a person who is loving, extremely loyal, and very honest. While, these are great characteristics to have, there is one problem: the wisdom of these characteristics is still growing, and it is apparent by this individual's actions which occasionally manifest in this person's online presence.

When we're in the middle of a test, that's not the time to shout out the answers that we think we know, complain about the test we're going through, or share on social media how we got in the class in the first place! It's normally quiet during a test, primarily for concentration, internal assessment and evaluation. When you're in the middle of a test or trial, it's not the time to share your process and journey on social media platforms. And, this is not to be deceitful, or perpetuate the conception that life is perfect, but to minimize outside opinions as you focus on passing your test, so you can graduate to the next level. Keep in mind a few things though: when we fail tests, we take them again and when we graduate, the tests increase in level of difficulty. There are no detours to this process. We simply grow and experience greater tests in life or we remain the same and find ourselves visiting the same frustrations over, and over, again.

There is never a definitive way or theory when dealing with social media, but Lady Wisdom should be your best friend. Wisdom should guide your written and verbal words that you share with others. She should be your focal point when engaging with family, friends, and associates, especially on social media.

2

RELATIONSHIPS MATTER

S ocial media is quite fascinating. My generation has witnessed online engagement grow from hours of playing SIMS, waiting for dial up, Myspace and BlackPlanet-- to Facetime, Snapchat and Marco Polo. Although millennials get a bad reputation for being disengaged from reality, we have mastered the social enhancement of online communities. We're unique in this perspective: generations before us were not fully engulfed into the Internet phase and generations after millennials do not know life without it!

Building relationships utilizing the power of social media takes more than simply adding someone you've met to your *friends list* or following someone who sent a random request. Social media should enhance relationships - not take the place of in-person connections. When used to its full potential, social media provides forums to shed light on social injustice around the world, it connects like-minded individuals who would not have connected otherwise, and it gives more options to expand connections beyond the ebbs and flows of our busy lives.

On the contrary, some individuals neglect the importance of in-person connection or genuine relationships outside of social media.

Written communication such as email, text messages, and social media posts eliminate important components that make up communication. Written communication removes eye-contact, tone, and body language. In essence, it removes visibility of the things that make us human.

To further confuse the process, our intent is at the mercy of the reader. Have you ever sent a message to someone when you were in a rush, and you decided to shorten the message through using abbreviations and minimal punctuation? Depending upon the mindset of the reader, that message could have been received in any number of ways. The reader may have sensed a tone of anger or apathy, or possibly attitude! This may not have been your intention behind the message, but since your non-verbal context clues are missing, the gaps are filled in by the recipient's imagination, mindset, and current feelings.

Although social connections are great, authentic relationships make social engagement much stronger and more fulfilling! Social media gives us the ability to connect with individuals all over the world, whom we may never connect with otherwise. We have a great opportunity to all become great storytellers through the digital platform of social media.

In the process of mastering social interaction and digital engagement, we neglect to keep the true foundation of communication. We forget to periodically call and check on friends and loved ones. In the workplace, when a miscommunication occurs, it is typically not our first mindset to pick up the phone or walk over to the individuals' desk we have conflict with for a face-to-face discussion. This must change. And, before we can change the world, a change must occur within. You've probably guessed it by now, this begins with you! If this is an area of current struggle for you, commit to initiating better face-to-face practices this week! Who knows? Your new habits just may have a positive impact on your coworkers and begin a ripple effect to bring back the art of in-person dialogue.

UNDERSTANDING THE HIGHLIGHT REEL

ACCORDING TO TIME MAGAZINE AND DELOITTE, RESEARCH finds that the average American between ages 18 and 24 looks at their phones with an average of 74 checks per day. Americans in the 25-34 age bracket look at their devices 50 times per day, and those 35-44 do so 35 times each day (TIME, 2015). Additionally, the average American checks their Facebook, Twitter, and other social media accounts 17 times a day, which equates to at least once (or more) every waking hour. Among all the social platforms, Facebook still dominates the space for most engagement, users, and effective algorithms. Immediately following is Snapchat, Twitter and Instagram.

Typically, people share upbeat posts daily. Often, someone on your *friends list* will share updates about his or her children, amazing vacations, job promotions, and exciting moments in life that encourage fans or *followers* to perceive that life is full of fun and adventure! Less shared are the realities of life:

- A newlywed couple experiencing a miscarriage
- Moments or seasons of depression
- The massive responsibilities and late hours that accompany a promotion
- The late feedings and consequential deliriousness that coincide with the beautiful gift of a newborn baby's life
- A failed marriage

The above list is a few examples of things that most people exclude from social media. Never get caught into the highlight reel and forget that social media only captures quick glimpses of a person's life.

The Social Media Comparison Lie

In addition to minimizing the other components of true communication (like body languages and tone), social media can become a powerful yet deadly platform for comparison. People associate success with number of likes, shares, and comments rather than staying focused on one's internal journey of fulfillment.

I had a friend whom I loved and adored. I always spoke so highly of her. I thought her life was perfect because social media gave off the perception that she had an amazingly loving husband, a beautiful child, friends and loved ones all around, a gorgeous home, and she appeared to have fun things to do every weekend! In my mind, she had it all.

It wasn't until one day while speaking with her on the phone, truth and reality set in. Her child was going through a phase of the terrible twos and she often felt alone because her husband worked odd, long hours. Her family was across the country and she missed her close siblings dearly. During that conversation, she also hinted to the idea that her marriage isn't 100% perfect-- just like all others.

The lens of comparison slowly moved away from my eyes. The idea of perfection that I subconsciously placed on another person began to shed away. Without realizing it, I played out the story of her life in my mind with no regard to life happening to all of us. I regretfully allowed the social media highlight reel to guide my thoughts into believing someone in this life had it all and was absent of problems.

We're all human. There is no such thing as perfection - only progress, and no one on this earth has it all together. We're all on a journey that requires grit, determination, and resilience. It also behooves us to have compassion, grace, and understanding toward each other along the way. No matter how great we think we are (or how great we want others to *think* we are), we're all one decision or circumstance away from the reminder that we're simply humans in need of grace.

Social media has deepened the wound of comparison for most. Prior to the ability to share and post all of life's amazing moments, we would actually have to call, write, or visit someone to learn how things were going. It took effort to stay in the know and because of that, there weren't many people on that list. Let's be honest! The amount of people we actually make effort to maintain real live contact with is drastically different from the number of friends or followers that we have on our social media profiles.

This isn't an accident. According to Dunbar's Theory, it has been proven that the brain can only nurture and maintain approximately 150 active relationships at a time. This doesn't mean that we don't have additional relationships, but it does imply that we can only properly invest in 150 or less. With the help of social media, the line of this has been blurred because of Facebook timelines, Instagram feeds, and Twitter updates. Without making any effort at all, we could find out relevant and current information on those we have the least interaction with.

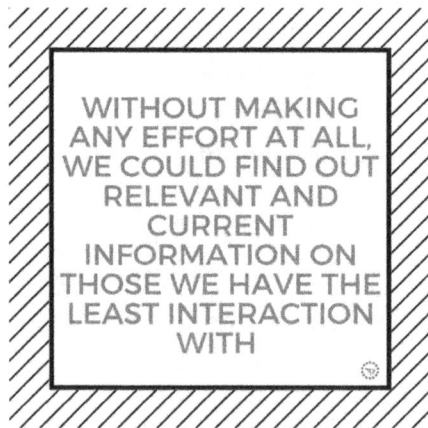

WITHOUT MAKING ANY EFFORT AT ALL, WE COULD FIND OUT RELEVANT AND CURRENT INFORMATION ON THOSE WE HAVE THE LEAST INTERACTION WITH

THIS GREATLY IMPACTS HOW WE VIEW OUR RELATIONSHIPS, TO what extent we feel effort is needed, and how close we truly are to a person. There is someone I attended high school with who I wasn't necessarily close to in grade school, but we decided to connect via Facebook anyway. We remained connected for years and over time, I noticed a shift in her posts. She went from frequent updates about the love of her life, to those posts becoming non-existent, as she began only sharing quotes. This could have been the product of my natural instinct to sniff out social trends in the marketplace, but chances are, if I noticed, others did too. To be clear, a separation notice was never posted; however, it was implied by what she was no longer sharing in her posts. Her silence and abrupt shift in communication spoke louder than any words shared on her profiles.

SILENCE CAN
OFTEN SPEAK
LOUDER THAN
WORDS.

IN A SITUATION LIKE THIS, SOME COULD ASSUME THAT SHE WAS over-sharing but not necessarily. She was simply doing what most people do, she is no different from any of us.

Reflect on your own social media presence, your cadence, and the things your talk about on your profiles. Are you perpetuating the idea of the perfect life?

Everything in life is about balance, including social media engagement and consumption. Be willing and open to the evolution of your extended branding platform, so it can help you to get closer to your dreams and goal.

———————

3

AND THE TWO SHALL BECOME ONE

THE SYNCHRONIZATION OF REALITY AND DIGITAL REALITY

"To be yourself in a world that is constantly trying to make you something else is the greatest accomplishment." Ralph Waldo Emerson

PICTURE THIS:

The night before her first day of high school, she picked out her best outfit, reviewed her schedule and tried to calm the nerves of excitement within her. She couldn't believe that she was going to high school and will soon be headed off to college in a few short years.

On the first day, it was nothing as she expected. The halls were crowded, her outfit become mediocre compared to the girls she saw walking the hallway, and no one seemed to care about the curriculum, yet alone the colleges they may attend. She quickly realized that if she wanted to seem likeable, she had to fit in. She couldn't show that she cared about her grades, loved modest clothing and already picked out the college she wanted to attend. To have friends, she had to be like them.

The next day, she approached her day a little differently. She changed into something more revealing in the bathroom before her classes and she left her backpack in her locker (taking only a pen and a notebook like the others). She decided to sit in the back and rarely spoke up. At home and internally she was one person, but to her peers and the student body, she was someone totally different.

This continued throughout her High School career. When it was time to apply to colleges, she was ready to go and discreetly asked one of her teachers to write her a letter of recommendation.

The teacher sat back amazed and pleasantly surprised. "You're planning to attend college? That's great! Can't say that I saw this coming. The folks you associate with don't seem to be that interested in college or their future."

"Oh." She stood there silently, shifting her weight to the other side of her body and trying her best to not make eye contact.

"I can write this for you, but I must be honest. Unfortunately, you've never spoken up in class, you're not a part of any extracurricular activities that I am aware of, and I don't know much about you outside of those you associate yourself with-- and well... that's it."

After the teacher's comment, her heart sank. She saw her friends in the hallway glaring her way with curiosity. Instead of voicing her truth and why the recommendation mattered to her, she briskly turned and walked out of the classroom, without a word to justify how she's different from the ones she surrounded herself with for the last four years.

THIS SEEMS LIKE THE CLASSIC HIGH SCHOOL STORY! RIGHT? WE have all fallen into peer pressure at some point in our lives. For whatever reason, we associated with the wrong people while trying to *fit in* with the majority. We failed to take time to discover our own, true voices because we were so busy imitating those around us.

Doesn't this scenario sound elementary? Now that we are adults and have experienced both good and bad real-life situations, this scenario may not seem so serious, at first glance. Well, it may sound like child's play, but this happens all the time. This occurs when our real lives are one way and we portray our lives in a completely different way on social media.

DON'T LOSE
YOURSELF
TRYING TO
BLEND IN.

THE BLURRED LINES BETWEEN REALITY AND THE IMPOSTER

IF SOMEONE RELIED SOLELY ON YOUR SOCIAL MEDIA PROFILES TO gain a first impression of you, what would he or she conclude about you? Would this person say you're funny, blunt, political?

Truly think about this for a moment.

After evaluating your social media profiles and creating an *idea* in his or her mind about the type of person you are, and then having an opportunity to meet you in person, what would this individual think? Will this person be completely baffled, confused or greatly pleased that who you were perceived to be is in fact who you are in real life?

If you're thinking, "I don't want anyone judging me and I don't care what people think of me," you're already off base for the point I am making. You're also in great denial about the truth when it comes to human nature. We all have personal thoughts and judgements about things, people and experiences. How we consider and challenge these judgements matter greatly in comparison to our usage of natural instincts to help us make sense of the world.

There are two sides to this: personal and business (and keep in mind these lines blur immensely as social media continues to evolve). From a personal perspective, the double lives can create unnecessary drama. From a professional standpoint, it can create a lot of uncomfortable situations and disappointing outcomes.

Are you aware that some jobs factor your social media presence in their final decision-making process on whether you're the right person for the role? Financial institutions can also decide to approve or deny a loan based upon your social media activity (along with the financial misconduct of your friends and followers). It doesn't seem fair, but they say birds of a feather flock together. One would assume that also applies to online social connections, right? You should be mindful of all this as you present yourself on social media. It all matters.

My main point is, BE YOU. Don't create a double life on social media and seem surprised or put off when people seem to feel a disconnect from you and your social presence. If you create this life online that's completely contrary to the actual life you live, you're doing yourself and the world a disservice. Among the approximate 6 billion people in the world, there is only one you. Own that and be as authentic and true to yourself as you possibly can.

How You want to be Perceived vs. How Others Perceive You

I KNEW THIS WOMAN WHO WAS PHENOMENAL AT HER JOB. SHE was extremely qualified for the role; she was a great writer, competent in her industry, had years of undergraduate and graduate level education to justify her ability to exceed in the job. However, there was this one off-putting thing about her. She was extremely rude. I wouldn't normally say this about a person, but it reinforces a point that must be clear. Her attitude went beyond a sporadic bad day. It was consistent - at any moment, she could present behavior that would shift the entire energy in a room.

Although her work was immaculate and her ideas for work were often great conversation starters, no one enjoyed working with her. She would gossip to coworkers about one another and completely throw people under the bus as needed - especially if it meant she wouldn't have to be accountable for an apology.

Her time with the company was very short lived. Not because of her work, but primarily because of her attitude. Since she failed to treat others with kindness throughout her career, her network was unwilling to endorse or recommend her for any future roles with other companies. It took her years to get back into her field, at the professional level and title she held before her departure.

I'm certain she didn't perceive her attitude and actions as the foundation of her problems but everyone else did. Even if she attempted to paint a different picture of herself toward others, the perception others had of her overruled her attempts.

Pure truth is always skewed by an individual's perception of reality, which is one of the many reasons why two people could live in the same household with the same parents yet perceive childhood experiences from completely different lenses.

When it comes to social media, the lens of perception and reality can truly build misconceptions of what is truth. Behind a computer screen, someone could create a facade of perfection that makes their lives look without struggle or adversity. Considering we all have battles to fight in life, this can't be further from the truth.

Don't believe the hype. It's not real! I have some interesting news to share: it was never intended to be a platform of reality. It was built for connectivity, with neither truth nor lies in mind. Social media by itself is merely a connecting tool. Without a user, it has no mind, no motive, and no positioning on life. Social media receives value and impact through people. It provides a bridge to connect the distance between former communication channels via Skype calls, Facebook videos, Tweets which contain 280 characters of information, and more!

The power of social media is in the hands of the person using it. You could use it to spread negativity and division, or you could maximize a message through influence and impact. The decision is completely yours.

Whatever your passion, I recommend you use it to build upon the things you love and find interest in. Although you cannot control the message conveyed by others, you have full control over the message you present to the world. That message will build a perception for someone, so be wise about the point of view you share and make sure you balance transparency with your authentic voice.

4

MAXIMIZE THE POWER OF YOUR PODIUM

BECOMING THE CHIEF OF YOU

Within an organization, the Chief Executive Officer is responsible for overseeing the vision and ensuring all decisions are strategically aligned with the core values and mission of the business. They often set the tone for all employees and maintain primary responsibility for the success or failure of the company.

Gary Cohen, associate dean of the Office of Executive Programs at the University of Maryland's Robert H. Smith School of Business and certified executive coach facilitated a TedTalk entitled, *You are the CEO of Your Life.* During his motivational monologue, Cohen encouraged his audience to recognize the power of personal brand ownership. To consider yourself the CEO of your life requires a strategic vision and personal accountability to accept that *we choose* our paths in life instead of allowing life to simply happen.

This role is primarily thought of within a business environment, but this also applies to one's life. We make executive decisions on who to marry, the careers we work, the clothing we wear, and the people we choose to have in our lives - mostly without purposeful approach or realizing the level of intention required. These are all choices we've decided to make based upon our personal-life compasses.

Would you consider yourself strategic with your life? How often do you outline financial goals, vacation planning, and career milestones that you would like to achieve?

Unfortunately, many people live in a reactive state of mind when it comes to life planning and personal ownership. After bills arrive, some wait until the last minute to pay them. We wait until a relationship is on life support before addressing deeply rooted problems, only to invest a quick fix solution instead of putting in the work to find the true essence of the issue we're facing. As life happens *to us*, we react with a victim mindset of *"this is happening TO me."*

Instead of taking a proactive approach to life, responsibilities, and happiness, most people choose to let life happen to them. It's as if they stand still as the universe simply flows all around them. This is no way to live! Allowing life to simply happen minimizes the beauty of living your best life. Become present *for you*. Begin to make declarations over your life through writing goals and speaking affirmations. The mind is the most powerful weapon on this earth. We can think ourselves into pity or self-doubt, or we can think ourselves into conquering our greatest fears and achieving our biggest dreams. Here is a great reminder:

---

*We cannot change the inevitable. The only thing we can do is play on the one string we have, and that is our attitude...I am convinced that **life** is 10% what happens to me and 90% how I **react** to it. And so it is with **you**...we are in charge of our attitudes."*

-Charles R. Swindoll

We have little to no control over the external variables that happen in life: a loss of a job, the death of a beloved family member or friend, natural disasters and unfortunate family circumstances are just a few examples of these things. No matter how hard we fight for control, these are the things in life that we must accept as the cards we're dealt with in our lives respectively. As a product of a broken home, I cannot control the separation of my parents-- but I can control how I allow the situation to impact me as a human being.

Life is about choices. We can choose to remain reactive toward life, get upset that things aren't happening the way we've planned, and allow life's events to sway us left and right. We can also choose to be proactive and strategic about our lives and goals. Becoming proactive in your life will require accountability, ownership, and grit. It will mean that no one can be blamed for the undesirable things that have occurred in your life. It also means you will take charge of becoming CEO of your own life.

> BE THE CEO
> OF YOUR LIFE,
> WITHOUT
> APOLOGIES.

In business, the Chief Executive Officer is responsible for overseeing the strategic vision and goals for the organization. They oversee the overall success of the company and can't allow minor details and setbacks to deter them from meeting annual expectations. They constantly find ways to improve processes and protocols to become more efficient and effective. They also bear all responsibility for their teams' actions. Great leaders lead by example and exemplify a heart of servitude. They ultimately understand the decisions they make impact more people than just themselves. These leaders take ownership and accountability for their actions and sometimes the actions of others. Envision governing your own life in such a way and then, act accordingly.

Are you up for the challenge? If so, become the CEO of *YOU*!

Understanding your Target Audience

Whether you're posting on social media on behalf of a company or to friends and family-- while speaking to an audience of five thousand or five people, understanding your audience is crucial to your influence. It's essential to the idea of people going beyond *hearing* your voice or seeing your written thoughts to digesting what you have to say.

Many times, people post their ideas, thoughts, and opinions not realizing that people can subconsciously pick up on the core energy behind the post and message. Beyond the intended message, you also have individuals that will perceive the content based upon their personal space and circumstances rather than the creator's motives. The further we get away from face-to-face communication, the more we become misguided in our ability to truly understand the full message behind the intended communication.

Have you ever sent an email or text message to someone and it was completely received out of context? When you drafted the message, you were sure the receiver would grasp your thoughts, not to mention, would appreciate the thoughtful approach in which you crafted your message with careful consideration of your tone. Well, they didn't.

Understand this occurrence has nothing to do with your intent. Although extremely convenient, a text message, direct message, or email can be taken completely out of context. This is beyond the control of the author and exists regardless of the author's intention.

There was a point and time in my life when I failed to understand the great importance of this concept. It was very early in my career and I was faced with a very difficult situation in the workplace. Instead of speaking to the person directly, I chose to send an email outlining my points and justification for my position. In addition to sending the email, I copied many people to the email for visibility. The recipient's response was the complete opposite of what I thought it would have been. As a result, we had a much larger issue that was never resolved until I left the department. During my final lunch with the executive director, she shared a piece of wisdom that I carry in my heart today:

"There is nothing better than direct communication. If something occurs that you do not agree with or you're unsure of the intent, speak to the person personally and be willing to have the difficult conversation. When doing this, know your audience. We cannot handle everyone the same. We must learn the best approach for the audience receiving the message."

WHEN COMMUNICATING YOUR POSITIONING, WHETHER IT BE TO a customer, a potential business partner, or a friend, understand your audience. Think of their perspective prior to the conversation, attempt to understand their motives and possible tensions during the discussion. This level of preparation can help you think of all angles while remaining empathetic to your audience.

SPEAK TO YOUR AUDIENCE IN A WAY THAT RELATES TO THEM.

Remember, relationships are most important. When we focus on the value of relationships, including the one we have with ourselves, a sense of genuineness remains present in everything you do. Start with an honest look at your motives, remain true to yourself, and be mindful of your communication style with others. This combination will maintain a realness that will be difficult for others to ignore.

5

THINKING BEYOND NOW

The content you share on social media becomes your digital fingerprint – it provides specific data for you to be digitally typecast. The updates shared begin to shape how family, friends, associates, and companies view you and your expressions of life's moments. It was always intriguing (and somewhat bothersome) to me when I would meet someone in person and then, look them up on social media, only to perceive a contrary persona from the person I just met! This is absolutely confusing! Which should people believe? Should we view the persona behind the computer screen or the person portrayed in the real world as your authentic self? Unless you're in the field of entertainment as an actor/actress or have a reason to have different lifestyle personas, it sends a clear superficial signal to those around you.

A genuine approach to social media begins with being true to who you are as a person. That requires self-reflection and being clear about your motives, intentions, insecurities, and setbacks. It's when you embrace all of you and allow yourself the permission to be beautifully flawed. I mentioned this before, but please know that this process doesn't require you to expose your soul on the internet, for all to see. Wisdom accompanied with transparency can create magical relationships that we crave to have in our everyday lives. Extending that level of maturity to social media can simply amplify your influence and impact.

Often times, superficial behavior can be sniffed out a mile away (by people, regardless of stature, or companies, regardless of size). This has more truth on social media, with consideration of the spammers, trolls, and bot accounts.

Inauthenticity within social profiles can also have a great impact on other areas of life, not just with how people perceive you, *socially*. If you're in the job market, employers will check your profiles. If you're in the market to buy a new car, some finance departments will vet your online presence with the assumption that surely those who are financially responsible will also be personally responsible on social media as well. There is no way of getting around it; not even private accounts. A private account is still searchable and depending upon the company's access to certain platforms and clearance level, private accounts are deemed reviewable as well.

While working at one organization, my team was responsible for vetting all social engagements and traffic. One morning, we received a tweet from an unknown person referencing a company employee and her questionable behavior on Twitter. Due to company policy, we were required to review the allegations and forward all information to human resources and her manager. Because of her choice to have a Twitter war, all the tweets were saved through a screenshot, sent to her employer, and eventually cost her employment with the company.

It sounds harsh, but in reality, you're representing someone else always. Whether it's with your parents, your family, your employer or yourself, your behavior *matters*. Online disagreements should never be worth misrepresentation of those you love or the things you've worked hard for. So, remember to pick your battles, as a matter of fact, try not to battle online at all, and as always, remember to choose your online communications wisely.

THE POWER OF OWNERSHIP

"Attack the evil that is within yourself, rather than attacking the evil that is in others."
— **Confucius**

Learning the power of branding ultimately resides in learning the power of ownership. To own your brand as a person and human being (with no regard to profession or personal attributes), it means to own your *authenticity*.

Many people are going through life with a victim mentality.

- They can't find a good job because no one has given them a break.
- They have a horrible attitude because many people have mistreated them in the past.
- They are unable to get out of debt because life keeps getting in the way.

Yes, life is unpredictable, full of ups and downs, and unforeseen circumstances that are beyond our control. However, while experiencing this thing called life, we're all given one thing: choice. We may be unable to control the things we go through, but we can choose how we respond to them. We can choose how we allow the experience to impact our perspectives. We can choose to see the good in all things and people—even in the worst situations.

When I went to college—like so many that come from single parent households, I had little financial support to help with funding my college education. I had a dream and a goal that I knew would manifest, but I had no idea how I would get there. To help get

31

through college, I decided to take out private student loans every semester. I knew I could get federal assistance but didn't have much guidance with filling out the form and the process to submit the form. Isn't that crazy? Or is it crazy... My story isn't an unfamiliar one and millions of college students and alumni in the United States can relate to this scenario of limited financial guidance while having direct access to Sallie Mae loans (without proper education of how the decision will impact them for years to come). According to the US Department of Education's Federal Student Aids' reports Americans owe over $1.48 trillion in student loan debt, spread out among approximately 44 million borrowers. At about $620 billion more than the total U.S. credit card debt, these statistics prove: *Surely, I wasn't the only one!*

Directly out of college, I didn't truly see the impact of my student loan debt. When signing on the dotted line, I didn't consider the other bills I would have as an adult that would be revolving doors of responsibility. Initially, I was in shock. I was fearful of what my future looked like. I thought, "How will I survive!"

Guess what; I'm surviving.

I attended graduate school and signed on the dotted line again-- but this time making the choice to **OWN IT.** I couldn't blame Auntie Sallie or her little brother Navient for being the only ones to believe in my dreams with investment. I couldn't curse the very thing that I was proud of any longer.

I made a choice to take ownership of my decisions, *all of them.*

Choosing to OWN our stuff is powerful! It removes the victim mentality and empowers you to freely live in your own boldness. It allows the world to experience an unapologetic version of yourself that could otherwise be hidden or ignored.

Be courageous and own the cards that you're dealt. In the process, you may help someone else do the same.

OWN THE
BRAND OF
YOU, LIKE YOU
MEAN IT.

CONCLUSION

Things in life will constantly change and evolve. There will always be new technology, cutting-edge innovation, and life-changing discoveries within the world. However, as the world changes with new technology and innovation, make the choice to remain grounded. Whether you're a small business owner or an individual who loves social media, never forget these things:

Stay connected to your foundation and know your *why* in life. Regardless of the change around you, understanding your "why" will keep you grounded throughout your life.

Relationships matter. Although a very powerful connector, social media can never take the place of human-to-human interaction. Make an intentional effort to ensure the people in your life feel your presence beyond digital check-ins.

Stay true to *YOU*. Imitating another person's life, gifts, or talents will not help you in anyway. There is only one *you* in this world; everyone else is taken. There is a divine purpose for your life and you're worthy of fulfilling that purpose. *So, do it.*

Own who you are unapologetically and with boldness. The world needs to see more originality and bravery. It's okay to be afraid but never let it stop you from moving forward. Hopefully, this book gave you inspiration, and great reminders to take care of your own brand along the way.

The second half of this book will be a resource guide to for entrepreneurs who know the importance of social media but struggle to find the "secret sauce" that drives performance goals and revenue.

If you're not a small business owner, I highly encourage you to keep reading. There are many complexities within the social media industry that general consumers rarely notice. The Social Media Small Business ToolKit may give you a glimpse into the business of digital and social mediums. Who knows... you may be inspired to turn your passions into a thriving business along the journey. If that happens, let's take the adventure together and be sure to take your *brandticity* with you!

THE BRANDTICITY

SOCIAL MEDIA SMALL BUSINESS TOOLKIT

As I wrote this book, I began to realize that although millions are on social media, the tips, tricks, and hidden gems of its impact is still unknown to the average consumer. Most social media users focus on the primary usage of the platforms without realizing the power of the platform, the impact of each post, and the lasting power of the decisions made regarding social media. It becomes a place to mentally dump ideas or vent instead of being used for its core purpose: *connectivity.*

Since this has become the norm, there are two extreme responses to the presence of social media and most people reside within one of these areas:

People either share too much or stay away from the platforms completely, because it's perceived as being a distraction and too personal for one's taste. Of course, if not approached with balance, it can become a negative thing in your life, but that's all dependent upon how you use it. As mentioned in a prior chapter, social media is completely useless without people. It's simply an electronic bridge between one person or a group of people to another.

WITHOUT PEOPLE LIKE US, SOCIAL MEDIA IS POWERLESS

Without people, it's completely useless.

Without the words, messages, and sentiment, there's nothing sharable.

Without authenticity, it becomes noise.

Without purpose behind the authentic words, it's a place where we share noise that resonates a diluted message that roams aimlessly.

Over the course of one year, I surveyed hundreds of small business owners within many different industries to determine *real-life* questions that many have regarding social media. Those questions and answers have been incorporated into this reference guide and I share it as a tool to help *you* navigate the social media landscape for your business.

Small Business Toolkit

FACEBOOK

Facebook is a social networking service launched on February 4, 2004. It was founded by Mark Zuckerberg with his college roommates and fellow Harvard University student Eduardo Saverin. With approximately 2.2 billion users as of December 2017, the Facebook platform is undeniably the most powerful social media engine in the world.

Originally, this platform was for college students only. It was a virtual connection tool for these students across the United States. As one of the first members on the platform, I recall using Facebook to connect with fellow college students around the East Coast (within driving distance from my university). We would connect on Facebook, share homecoming dates, and make new friends during homecoming visits. You may perceive this as dangerously risky, but this was the purpose of the platform: connecting people around the world.

Many students I've connected with years ago are still on my Facebook Friends List and it has been wonderful to see our journeys evolve along the way. Given personal experiences like these, coupled with my professional experience in social media marketing, I have assessed the following information. May this toolkit enhance your understanding and enlighten your perspective.

Frequently asked Questions from Small Business Owners

Does Facebook even matter to my marketing strategy?

Of course, it does! With the platform having 2.2 billion active users, you have an opportunity to reach a wide range of people that are interested in the services and products that you provide. Social media is constantly changing, but it's definitely here to stay. Do not count yourself out of the game by eliminating one of the most powerful current social media engines to date.

To make a brand profile, you must have a personal account. So, this means, you will need to have an actual Facebook page to then build your brand page. If you're not keen on sharing your personal life on social media, don't worry! Here's a little trick: you can always create an unused account that will grant you access to create and manage a Fan/Brand page. For example, create an account and build a very small circle of friends-- which should be connected to your brand to keep the page discreet. Do not add an image for your main picture. Place all your focus on the creation of your brand page. For those that are very active users on Facebook, this part has become one of the main difficulties for managing a brand and a personal page: balance. How do you know when to share on your personal page versus your brand page? When can your personal content make a negative impact on your brand? If you're ever in doubt, do not post. If you ever need to choose between which plat-form to focus on, pick your brand. Build the empire for your brand and use the platform of social media to further reach your goals. It's always great to converse with others, but make it a point to further establish your professional brand to new potential clients and consumers.

What is Facebook Advertising and do I need it?

When Facebook opened its platform to the public, it allowed for all people, regardless of status, or collegiate attendance to join the network. This was also true for brands and public figures. Those who were smart jumped on board immediately. Their proactivity and willingness to take the risk paid off in their number of followers to date.

Nowadays, it's nearly impossible to gain followers organically on the platform. Why you ask? Numerous reasons impact this:

- User customization of timelines
- Ability to *Like* a page but *Unfollow* the updates
- Facebook's algorithms tailor more to friends and recent searching topics by the users

All this doesn't work in favor of organic reach for brands. As a result, Facebook advertising is a must to gain traction on the platform! You don't need a large budget to make great impact. Start with a small monthly budget and be consistent in posting your messaging and content. You can also begin by simply boosting current posts to test the waters. It will provide you the basic version of Facebook advertising, but it will help you to see the impact and value of your dollars on the platform.

FOR BUSINESSES, FACEBOOK ADVERTISING IS REQUIRED TO REACH YOUR AUDIENCE.

What's the best way to boost a post for my brand?

As you start off with your Facebook promotions, you can simply begin by boosting your posts directly from the platform. By doing this, you can choose your top line targeting parameters or keep a general audience. This is the *simplest* way, yet not the most effective. When you boost a post, you're not able to truly tap into your core audience or demographic.

This lends me to remind you to *know your audience*. Be mindful of who you want to connect with and who will most likely connect with your company. Many people will say, "I want to appeal to the mass population." That's great, however, there is no clear direction for your messaging in that way. For example, I have a very soft spot in my heart to help women entrepreneurs fulfill their dreams. I can say that I want all women to resonate with my posts, which means I'm focusing on women vs. men, but how I communicate my message to a 45-year old woman should be very different from how I relay the same message to a 21-year old woman. Their mindsets, goals, and core tensions will not be identical. So, it is vital to take this into consideration while promoting on social media, especially via Facebook.

To tap into a more detailed structure of crafting your audience for the platform, you need to log into your account through *Facebook Business Manager* (more details on this shortly). This is a totally different website that provides access to the backend of your accounts for your business pages. Through Business Manager, you're able to review page analytics (how well your content is doing), review the best days to post content according to your audience, and build your targeting parameters.

What are targeting parameters?

Targeting parameters is another way of placing or creating guardrails around how you plan to reach your core audience or customer. Many small business owners believe it's best to sell their product to a very wide audience.

"If I isolate someone, I fear I will neglect a possible customer. So, I market to a general consumer and keep my possibilities open."

This is indeed the wrong thinking! Although it's easy to assume it's better to market your goods and products to the general population, the lack of focus in terms of messaging will essentially destroy your chances with truly resonating with your audience.

Targeting parameters isn't a Facebook or platform thing. It's a basic strategic marketing thing. Create a clear focus on who you serve with your goods or services and don't be afraid to walk away from business that doesn't align with that audience.

For example, I am the co-founder for an online boutique called NicholeNicole Vintage Boutique (Check it out at www.nicholenicole.com). When we first launched we decided that our audience would be women, late twenties, wives and moms. Within this demographic, many women experience a huge issue with shopping for clothing. These women want to look fashionable without the loss of modesty or comfort. Our goal is to help close this gap and become the boutique for every working mother, fabulous stay-at-home mom, newly married wife and late twenty somethings that want to look great, comfortable, and classy!

In the process of marketing our boutique to friends and family during our beta testing, many of our younger family members complained about our pricing model. They said it was too high. Well, we refused to budge on our pricing model. Not because we wanted to push against their feedback, but because we knew they were not a part of our core audience. This doesn't mean others that don't fit into your core audience won't want to shop or do business with you. It simply means that your messaging can be tailored to speak directly to a core group of people who resonate with your brand --- while you openly embrace others outside your target audience who have become interested in what you are doing.

Your understanding towards your audience matters. It will help you properly target and create your parameters for social media advertising.

What's the best way to manage paid posts on Facebook? Where do I even begin?

Before I begin to answer this question, I would like to point out one thing. Most of the information shared in this section is not accessible for everyone's online usage. The average consumer has no interest or value in this information, therefore these consumers may not have access to many of these resources provided by the Facebook platform.

> *To gain access to this type of data, you must have a business page on the platform and spend money for paid promotion.*

This is one of the most common questions I've received regarding the Facebook platform. Although the "boost post" button is extremely convenient and most appealing, it's not the most ideal way to manage your paid media posts. Facebook has another platform called *Facebook Business Manager*. It's a free account that is associated with your business accounts to assist you with managing paid media, targeting, analytics, and more, all in one place! Business admins can either access accounts via desktop or the *Facebook Ads App* for mobile access. Within the Business Manager platform, you can use your business targeting goals to build customized audiences that are most likely wanting to receive and engage with your content.

Additionally, through *Facebook Business Manager*, there is a wide range of resources that are instrumental to the success of your business.

Source: Facebook Business Manager Admin Page

Here are some of the most prominent sections where you should spend most of your time:

Business Manager - This is a section dedicated to providing an overview of advertising activity and key results across your advertising accounts and pages.

Why should I care?

This section will give you a topline view of your performance, how much you've spent per post, total engagements, cost per engagement or action (CPE or CPA),

Ads Manager - Ads manager gives you a deeper dive into your advertising campaigns (or posts). It's also another place to build and create advertising or paid posts for analysis of your performance.

Why should I care?

This will most likely be the place you spend most of your time as you create and build your paid posts. Although Business Manager provides you similar tools, this section is more in depth regarding your results, which can help you improve with future campaigns.

Audience Insights - This section provides deep insight into the people that matter most: your consumer or audience.

Why should I care?

Beyond page likes and posts reactions (likes, comments, and

shares), Audience Insights will give you an inside look at your audience. You can learn age demographics, purchasing behaviors, geographic locations, shopping/spending habits, the percentage of people that's connected to your brand that is also in the market for big purchases, and more. Sounds scary and insane that all this information can be found on a social platform, right? This goes back to my sentiments earlier; Be mindful of what and how you share on social media. This information isn't simply gathered by Facebook. There are many advertising partners that work together to compile this information to help businesses formulate smart business goals and marketing strategies.

Think of what you Google, in public and in private. All your searches help compile this fantastic information for marketers to use for better marketing practices and tactics, all with the intent that you will become a loyal fan or advocate for their brand.

Please do not be fooled: nothing on your phone is private and all things are traceable when the right people know how to search for them.

Analytics - In this section, marketers and business owners can review the success and areas for improvement with Facebook and Instagram ads.

Billing and Payments – Keep track of your billing, payments, currencies, taxes, and line of credit information in this section. Yes, all this is available via Facebook Business Manager!

YOU CAN CREATE
AND MANAGE
BOTH FACEBOOK
AND INSTAGRAM
ADVERTISING
WITHIN FACEBOOK
BUSINESS
MANAGER.

Facebook essentially wants your media to be successful, so the more impactful your message and content resonates with your audience, the more the platform serves the posts to like-minded consumers and the further your dollars will go for you on the platform.

How do you make payments for your ads on Facebook?

Have I mentioned that social media changes rapidly and it's critical that you commit yourself to be a continual student? As I am writing this book, Facebook announces its plan to test two timelines: one for friends, and family connections and the other timeline dedicated to exploring brands and other content.

As a consumer, this is great news! Content on a user's feed will feel more like the "old days" of Facebook and users will have the option to explore brands as they choose. For a business, this makes the importance of branding and paid targeting no longer a recommendation, but a requirement to reach your core audience.

Organic content will only reach approximately 1-3% of your fan base on the Facebook platform (your page fans and followers). The only way organic reach can go beyond your fanbase is through shares, which amplifies your reach. However, there is no way to "boost" your content for shares (excluding a direct call to action for your fans in your post copy).

As mentioned, this is a beta test currently happening (dating October 2017). No one knows when or if it will go wide to all users, but we should all be prepared for this, should it occur.

INSTAGRAM

Instagram launched in 2010 and joined the Facebook family in 2013. Although its own separate platform to users, the Facebook and Instagram platforms have the same operating systems when it comes to business. Within recent years, Facebook has made a great priority to streamline how businesses can manage advertising campaigns. Now, Facebook and Instagram advertising can all be managed through Facebook Business manager.

Instagram is a visual platform that maximized the power of hashtags (which originally started with Twitter-- to be discussed later). Pictures matter more than anything on this platform.

In addition to great visuals, the platform allows for Boomerangs and videos through the app, timeline experience and through its newest feature, IGTV, which enables content creators to upload content to the platform.

Wait...what's a Boomerang?

Think of the actual toys that we would play with as kids (well, some of us that grew up in the 80's and before). Boomerangs on social media have essentially the same concept but with video. A brief image simply loops and repeats itself (in retrospect).

How can I build my following on the platform? Is it similar to Facebook, since it's owned by Facebook?

Although Facebook owns Instagram, the platforms are very different in nature and approach. Facebook is becoming more of a "pay to play" platform for businesses and it's slowly transitioning this model to Instagram-- but don't fret! The platform still has great power for organic reach and engagement. This means that your efforts are not in vain, even if you don't have a lot of money supporting your posts as advertisements.

The best way to increase your following is to work with the engagement on the platform. You can do this is a very simple way: once you post, *get to work!*

Many people and brands tend to post on Instagram and leave the posts alone, watching it with fingers crossed that people will see it and engage with it. This is a very passive approach to a process that is very much engaged.

Once your image is posted, go to your heart and click the following tab to see the latest interaction from your followers. The recent interactions are often seconds from when you checked for the update. This tells you that the person is on the platform interacting right now! So, go to their profile and engage with their content:

- Like their photos
- Leave thoughtful comments on their posts
- Engage with the comments within their photos (which will notify the person who commented and give you added exposure)

Hashtags on Instagram:

Everyone talks about hashtags, but specifically on Instagram, they are living, breathing content lanes for engagement and connecting with an audience that is like-minded in nature.

What do I mean by this?

When you post a photo on Instagram with hashtags, your post could receive a lot of engagement from others if you put your hashtags to work! After your image is posted, the work is just beginning. Take the time to click each hashtag you've used to interact with other people on the platform. Here are the steps to do this:

- Click the hashtag for your post
- Click the first image that appears in the hashtag search

- Double click the image to give it an Instagram heart
- Scroll down and repeat the previous action for all photos you consider "worthy" of the heart
- Periodically leave a comment on photos that align perfectly with your brand (do not go overboard with this or make your comment too generic)
- Go back to your photo
- Click your next hashtag for your post
- Repeat this process

The ideal window of time is immediately after you've posted your image. That's the time you can really ramp up your posts engagement through hashtag engagement. However, if time simply doesn't permit for that immediate action, you can always use this method to find new people and introduce your brand to others who may not interact with your brand otherwise.

HASHTAG DISCOVERY DOES NOT HAVE TO APPLY TO JUST THE HASHTAGS YOU PUT ON YOUR POST! YOU CAN SEARCH ANY HASHTAGS AND ENGAGE WITH OTHERS ON THE PLATFORM ANYTIME.

Additionally, hashtags can be incorporated into your profile bio and you can actively follow hashtags as you do with people. Use this feature to your advantage! Follow the hashtags that matter most to your brand and engage with posts as you see them.

Can I share posts from my followers on the platform?

Instagram's platform does not have a "share" option for Timeline updates within the platform. You can save the posts, copy the link, and embed the photos but you cannot click a share button like other platforms. A great work around involves a third-party app of your choice that's designed to repost from Instagram profiles.

As of June 2018, you can now begin sharing Instagram Stories *if you're tagged in the original Story feature.* This could potentially be testing ground for the platform to have a "share" button in the near future.

Can I schedule posts with this platform?

Yes, you can! The platform's API allows for organic posts to be scheduled through third party scheduling tools. These types of tools include Hootsuite, Spredfast, Sprout Social, and others. The one you decide to use is truly a personal preference. I would recommend doing your research on your options to discover which works best for you and your business needs.

Scheduling platforms, like those mentioned can help you with almost every social media site when it comes to scheduling and time management. For example, Hootsuite can assist you with managing Facebook, Twitter, Instagram. LinkedIn, YouTube, Pinterest, and more!

SCHEDULING TOOLS ASSIST WITH CONSISTENCY AND TIME MANAGEMENT.

TWITTER

Twitter's platform was officially established in 2006 by Jack Dorsey and co-founder, Evan Williams. This was in an era when wireless plans charged for everything, including your "IN" network. So, the purpose was originally to build another form of communication for friends that was like texting, but web-based, and confined to a short character limit. The platform took off during a 2007 South by Southwest Conference, receiving over 60 thousand tweets per day. Now, it's one of the most prominent platforms that people think of when addressing social media.

What does the increase in character limits mean to me?

Well, aside from the obvious use of more characters, users now have more liberty for expression within the platform. I would keep in mind that although you have the additional characters, the length of your tweet doesn't matter as much as your impact, and overall messaging. If you don't have those two things, you tweet will be meaningless to your followers regardless of its length,

Is Twitter still valuable?

The Twitter platform is still alive and well! There has been speculation of this platform falling by the wayside for many years, and yet it's still prominent and extremely useful. It's important to recognize that every platform is different, and users go to each for several reasons, information, and functionalities.

One of Twitter's prized possessions is the real-time engagement during real life situations and events. Twitter took off when people went to Twitter to share their feelings during highly prominent shows or crucial events like the presidential elections. Instead of screaming thoughts at the television, people would blast feelings and reactions on the Twitter platform.

The social medium went beyond digital as people began hosting Twitter parties for their favorite season premieres or sporting events. When it comes to instantaneous information, Twitter takes the lead among all others.

Engagement, conversation, and availability matter most on this platform. On average, consumers expect a response from brands on social media within two hours of reaching out to them! It seems very demanding yet the day and era we live in revolves around instant gratification and on the spot results. When building a presence on Twitter, keep the standard two-hour response in mind and focus on building a relationship with your audience through engagement and online conversations. This will get you very far on Twitter in addition to the other platforms.

Many brands focus more on building conversations through the channel of customer service on the Twitter platform than any other. The real-time updates play a huge role in this and when handled properly, will build instant credibility and loyalty among your audience, customers, and peers.

Is it true that I can tweet the same messaging repeatedly?

Yes, this is true! The primary reason for this revolves around the constant stream of information and updates on a user's Twitter timeline. Think about it this way: if your customer has 300 active Twitter followers and you tweet a message at 10 a.m., your customer will see your update at that time, along with all other followers that may have posted at or around that same time. As new tweets come into a person's timeline, the older tweets are pushed down to filter in the new ones. This is all in real-time! Because of this, the lifespan of a tweet is 18-24 minutes.

One thing also worth noting revolves around knowing your audience. Some of your audience will be more engaged and active on the platform in the morning, some around noon, and others during the evening hours. These audience groups will have different types of consumption behaviors. So, learn the engagement behaviors of your followers and feel confident in sharing multiple tweets about one core message, to resonate with the various audience groups that will follow you on the platform.

What happens if I make a mistake on a tweet? Can I edit them?

Unfortunately, there is no editing ability to a Tweet. You must delete and post the corrected tweet in its place. The quicker you catch any potential mistakes the better. Knowing this, please be mindful that once a tweet is public on the platform, it is forever captured. One can recall the message through screenshots as it appears on the timeline. There is no such thing as a tweet that's gone forever. This is where the authenticity of your message, clarity in tone, and of course proofing requirements matter most.

What are my messaging limitations on the platform?

Prior to 2017, a composed tweet allowed for 140 characters, including spaces (not including embedded images, videos or handle mentions within the tweet). As of September 2017, news was released that the platform announced that they were testing the extension of the character limit from 140 to 280, including spaces. As a result, users now have more characters to express themselves. It was essentially in consideration for other languages that require more written text.

Twitter has the most restrictions on copy length—but at times this can be a wonderful thing. It requires one to thoroughly think through the message with clarity and precision. It forces you get to the point already!

Besides updating messaging with Tweets, what else can I do on the platform?

Twitter has many features that are greatly underutilized yet extremely useful when a person or brand takes advantage of them.

POLLS

Within business, brands would pay hundreds and thousands of dollars to gain insight from their audience or consumers. A business would build a survey through a surveying company or platform and even pay for the real input from people through focus groups. All that is great but when you're just starting off, what are some things that can be done within a tight budget? Twitter Polls! With Twitter, you can provide a poll to your audience for FREE. You can have four options within your poll and can extend the life of your poll through Twitter advertising.

The default time frame for a poll is one day, however, you can extend this up to 7 days.

TWITTER LISTS

As you're building your brand, remember, it's important to become a lifelong student at your craft. Things are always evolving, so, maintaining a studious mindset will keep you aware of the latest news in your industry and among your peers, while revealing potential ways to keep you ahead of the curve.

Twitter Lists are a way to organize those you follow by various topics and categories, all of which are up to you! For example, as a boutique owner, my business partner and I must stay on current trends. Here are some of our lists topics and categories:

Fashion influencers (any and everyone we deem inspirational within the fashion industry)

News Outlets (potential reporters, digital magazines, and bloggers that feature news on fashion boutiques, entrepreneurs, and off-the-beat style trends)

Competitors (any boutiques that are "like us." This list is great to keep an eye on what competitors are doing and how we measure up to their impact on the platform)

Inspiration (entrepreneur leaders, motivational speakers, and industry leaders for business success)

Another great thing about the Twitter lists: it's your choice to have them private or public! Private lists can only be viewed by the owner of the Twitter profile. This means, no one will be able to see your private lists unless provided admin access to your platform account.

Again, Twitter has so many great things to offer and provide to its 330 million monthly, unique users and still provide a great user experience.

If someone has the name that I want to use on the platform, what can I do?

It is highly recommended that once you have your business name in mind, do not wait to reserve your social media presence on each platform, especially Twitter. The platform is essentially a global platform and usernames are created consistently. Once they're gone—they're gone. Many times, it's extremely difficult to attain a name that is already in use. A brand can reach out directly to the user to request the name change, buy the username (or entire profile), or contact Twitter support for their guidance. The Twitter team does not step into these matters often unless there is a legal violation, such as a trademark, patent, or any other legal defilement by the current user.

If you're just starting off, do this now! Do not wait until you're ready to build your social media presence. If you reserve the usernames, you can always make the accounts private until you're ready to provide full dedication to the pages. Just don't wait.

How can I build followers on this platform?

The best way to build followers on Twitter is to engage, engage, and engage! Twitter is like a global virtual conversation with millions of topics and conversations happening all at once. It can be overwhelming or distracting for those who are unclear of how to incorporate their brand into the current tweets happening in real time.

Picture this:

You're invited to one of the largest networking events in the world (TWITTER). The event will have people from different industries, expertise, and walks of life. Additionally, all attendees of the networking event are welcome to bring their own friends (FOLLOW-ERS) to join the event's festivities and topics of discussion (TWITTER TIMELINE).

You're excited and ready to attend with the best intentions! You walk into this event, and there are millions of people in the room-- 330 million to be exact. You look around and you see no familiar faces but hear a wide range of topics, some conversations are much louder than others, which gets the attention of other people in the room who gravi-tate to the conversation. This makes the conversation louder and stronger (TRENDING TOPICS). You hear all this, but you have your own message you want to share so you start talking (A TWEET). Unfortunately, no one joins in or hears you due to the buzzing conver-sations happening all around you. So, you decide to try again and still no luck.

After some time, you decide to browse the room (TWITTER MOMENTS). There's a lot of interesting -- and random-- conversa-tions happening! You hear one that's intriguing to you and you notice people simply join in by blurting out their perspectives, ultimately making the conversation more powerful in the room. You join in and blurt out your thoughts and a few people look your way and smile (FAVORITE). A few others repeat your words as confirmation (RETWEET). Someone walks up to you and taps you on the shoulder.

"Hey, I loved your perspective on this. We should connect." (DIRECT MESSAGE)

You recognize your thoughts were amplified and something clicks for you...

For this event, collective conversation that's unplanned and sporadic makes magical moments that become amplified. Alone, your thoughts go unheard but when joined with others through the flow of immediate spurts of thought, the event's power comes to life.

Simply tweeting out messages on this platform is pointless. It will get you very little return on your time and effort. To maximize the power of this platform, you must think of how to incorporate your brand into current ongoing conversations while proactively connecting with other users. If you tweet about a brand, tag them by using the @mention. If you're a part of an event, follow the official hashtag and engage with others that are attending as well. If you're watching a show that aligns with your brand, share the experience by tweeting during the show, engaging with others who are watching as well, and using the official hashtag. All these things will help broaden your exposure on the platform and make you more visible to others.

Here are some key definitions you should consider when using the platform:

Follow: To follow on Twitter means you are subscribing to their Tweets as a follower. Their updates will appear in your Home timeline. That person can send you Direct Messages.

@ (at) Mention: also considered replies to a user by mentioning his or her username with the @ sign.

DM (Direct Message): these are messages on the platform that go directly into a private inbox to the user. Remember these can be taken as screenshots, so always remember nothing is truly private on the internet or with social media.

Tweet: simply the post update for Twitter.

Retweet: reposting a tweet or "post" from another user.

As you dive into Twitter, stay conversational, relatable, and authentic! It is truly about conversation and connecting with others on the platform as things are happening.

Live engagement will be one the best ways to spark engagement on your profile. If you're attending an event or conference, engage with others live using the official hashtag. At the moment, Twitter is the only platform that's lucrative for constant updates to your followers. Use that to your advantage during your next event.

PINTEREST

This social media platform is considered one of the most adored, newest, and yet the most confusing to business owners. Pinterest is an online gathering place for people to discover and share like-minded content such as recipes, fashion ideas, life tips and more!

The pinners feed is built through connections. The more people or boards a pinner follows, the more diverse and full the Pinterest feed becomes. It's all about the connections that drive the type of pins seen and shared.

The Art of a Pin

Pins consist of a few key things that make them impactful, shareable, and essentially powerful.

COMPELLING IMAGE: Very similar to Instagram, Pinterest is all about the visual look of your pictures. Be sure to make your picture look great and natural. Highly stylized images could actually have an adverse effect with users because it can come off as an advertisement instead of a sharable pin.

PIN DESCRIPTION: The description that's included with the pin should be short and to the point. Moment of truth: unlike a Facebook post, very few pinners read the descriptions. Because of this, don't waste precious time trying to be creative and witty with your written content on this platform.

PICTURE LINK: One of the great things about Pinterest centers around the fact that users are encouraged to click off the platform. That's right! With each pin, it should drive pinners to the source of the pin. The source can be a blog, recipe details, and especially an e-commerce site!

HAVE YOU TRIED: Pinterest has this great feature for users to mark things as "tried" if they attempted to recreate the pin in their everyday lives. This increases the power of a pin via recommendations and real-life confirmation that the pin is useful to the pinners.

Pinterest is very similar to Instagram in terms of the importance of a compelling visual. It's all about the picture. Text and descriptions do not have the same level of value. This simply means place your focus on your image, not the description of your picture.

Another thing worth noting is the associated link with your pin. As mentioned above, Pinterest is one of the few social media platforms that encourages the user to *click off the platform*. This is a huge deal! This means your associated link matters and if you're looking for website traffic, Pinterest may help you get it!

Is it true you can promote your pins?

Absolutely! All social media platforms now have some sort of paid advertising associated for businesses. If you have an ecommerce website, Pinterest can be your happy place when it comes to direct sales from a social media platform. According to Pinterest data, Pinners are 10% more likely to purchase items they pin than any other social website. So essentially, pins can translate to an impact on your bottom line: revenue.

The actual process is quite simple:

1. Pick a Pin. Promote your best Pins so they appear in the most relevant places.
2. Decide who sees it. Set up targeting so the right people see your Promoted Pin.

3. Choose your objective (for example, your objective can be engagements or website clicks).
4. Track what's working. Once your campaign starts, see how it's doing and make changes. To learn more, go to https://ads.pinterest.com/.

Would I see a quick return on promoting my pins?

Like all social media, you will need strategy and patience to do this correctly. Create a strategy for your promoted pins and give your strategy time after implementation to see if it proves successful. Time is not deduced to be one month, and it may not even be 6 months. Therefore, it is better to simply become diligent in tracking progress and conversion rates consistently.

If you're hoping for immediate results on your promoted pins, you will either need to adjust your expectations or invest in another platform that can meet your immediate need for your return on investment.

Do you need a lot of followers on Pinterest to be successful?

Absolutely not! Unlike the other platforms, the number of followers does not dictate the success of your pins. For example, on my Pinterest profile, I have approximately 500 followers. This isn't massive. However, I receive over 8K views per month on my pins collectively.

Additionally, originality is not necessary for your pins. Focus on great re-pins and sprinkle in your own content in the process! This will help your uploaded visuals to gain traction and *shareability*.

For this platform, focus on sharing content from others. Your profile growth will come through collaborative sharing.

IN A NUTSHELL:

Please know that all the questions and answers in the *Brandticity Social Media Small Business Toolkit* shed light on the surface of capabilities and features of social media. The truth is apps like Instagram, Pinterest, Facebook and Twitter evolve everyday with new features and updates, so be willing to learn and grow *with* these platforms.

If there comes a point that you feel as if you've mastered something, consider that a red flag and an indicator to discover the latest changes.

Social media is here to stay, and it will continue to change. Flow with the changes and enjoy the journey of learning!

————————

FINAL THOUGHTS

Words cannot express my gratitude for you choosing to invest in this book. Thank you! I truly hope this book helps you professionally and personally. I would like to personally thank each individual who took the time to share questions for each platform. I appreciate your willingness to learn and be a part of this experience.

Everything I do is centered around relationships and encouraging others to be the best they can possibly be during their beautiful time spent on earth.

This book is simply another extension of those efforts.

I will continue to expand on this book with new additions, revisions, and special editions. I hope that you will join me on the journey of being a continual student of this thing we call social media and digital marketing.

If you have any questions that you would like to be included in the next edition or topic/platform suggestions, reach out to me directly via my website: www.altimesenichole.com.

Altimese Nichole

LET'S CONTINUE LEARNING TOGETHER

Additional Resources for Entrepreneurs

Learn more about each platform and more at
altimesenichole.com

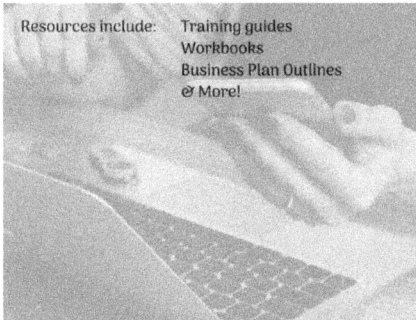

Resources include: Training guides
Workbooks
Business Plan Outlines
& More!

Altimese Nichole
ENTERPRISE, LLC

ABOUT THE AUTHOR

Altimese Nichole was born in Washington DC and raised in Virginia. She attained her undergraduate degree in Mass Communications, Broadcast Journalism from Virginia Commonwealth University and completed her Master of Management degree from the University of Phoenix. She has worked in public relations and marketing field for approximately 9 years with reputable global brands in Metro Atlanta. She currently leads the social media department for a highly recognized creative agency that represents notable brands across America.

Her passion resides in helping others, especially women pursue their dreams. With her expertise in public relations, branding, and social media, your brand will flourish with originality and authenticity.

She is a devoted wife and mother, and they reside in Hilton Head Island, SC.

www.altimesenichole.com
https://www.linkedin.com/in/altimesecurry/

facebook.com/AltimeseNicholeBranding

twitter.com/AltimeseNichole

instagram.com/AltimeseNichole

pinterest.com/AltimeseNichole